Name

Pet's name

Age

Birthday

Best friend

Favourite food

Favourite TV programme

Favourite sport

Brownie
Annual 2005

Brownie fun

Being a Brownie is great fun! Brownies do all sorts of exciting activities as part of their Brownie Adventure.

Stay safe

You should be able to have a go at everything in your great Brownie Annual 2005, but sometimes it's wise to ask an adult you know for help. You can still do it by yourself, just make sure the adult says it's okay and is watching.

Safety symbol

On some pages you'll see this symbol, to remind you that you might need a bit of help with the activity. If there isn't a symbol but you're still not sure, ask for help anyway.

Be safe

Badge link

On most pages of this great Brownie Annual 2005 there's a badge link. This shows that the ideas and activities on that page link to a Brownie badge. If you want to find out what you need to do to get the badge, look it up in the Brownie Badge Book. Remember when you do a badge, always do your best.

BADGE LINK

Craft
GLUE

Brownie Promise

I promise that I will do my best:
To love my God,
To serve the Queen and my country,
To help other people
and
To keep the Brownie Guide Law.

Your special Brownie saying

Lend A Hand

Brownie Law

A Brownie Guide thinks of others before herself and does a Good Turn every day.

My Brownie web safe code

When using the world wide web I promise:

★ to agree rules with my parents or guardians about the best way for me to use the computer and the world wide web.

★ not to give out my home address or phone number without permission.

★ not to give out the name or address of my school without permission.

★ not to agree to meet anyone who I contact on the web, unless my parents or guardians say it is all right and go with me.

★ not to put my photograph onto a web site.

★ to tell my parents, guardians, teacher or Guider if I find something on the web that worries or upsets me.

With thanks to the Girl Scouts of the USA for the ideas contained within this warning for children.

Web safe

Sixer tips

When you see this sign, you will find hints and ideas for things you could do with your Six at Brownie meetings. Why not suggest them to your Brownie Guider or talk about them in a Pow-wow?

Contents

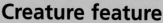

All illustrations and photographs as acknowledged on appropriate pages

The Brownies who appear in this Annual are from the 10th Clapham Hill Brownie Pack and the 5th Tooting St. Boniface Brownie Pack.

Special thanks to: Maria-Lourdes Lobo; Mary Day; Marion Thompson; Amanda Bailey at the RSPCA; missdorothy.com Ltd.; Sue Walmsley-Smith at the Fairtrade Foundation; Dan Ross and Hannah Graves at Victoria Foods; Colwyn Griffiths.

Written by Alison Smith apart from: *Beautiful butterfly*, *Brazilian bites*, *Chocs away!* and *Food glorious food* by Catherine Slater; *Miss Dorothy* by Wendy Watts at missdorothy.com Ltd. *The Grand Raffle* written by Kate Fenning.

Cover photographs by Laura Ashman.
Brownie photographs by Laura Ashman.

Brownie Annual 2005: an official publication of Girlguiding UK.
© The Guide Association 2004.

All Brownie and Guide photographs © The Guide Association.
Other photographs © as acknowledged on appropriate pages.

Published by Girlguiding UK
17-19 Buckingham Palace Road
London SW1W 0PT

Girlguiding UK is an operating name of The Guide Association.
Registered charity number 306016.
Incorporated by Royal Charter.

Girlguiding UK Trading Service ordering code 6005
ISBN 0 85260 210 3

Readers are reminded that during the lifespan of this publication there may be changes to Girlguiding UK's policy, or legal requirements, that will affect the accuracy of information contained within these pages.

Patron HM The Queen
President HRH The Countess of Wessex
Chief Guide Jenny Leach
Brownie Adviser Sue Waller
Project Editor Alison Smith
Project Designer Heather Peters
Designer Mary Ikoniadou
Cover Designer Heather Peters
Production Les Girling
Colour repro InTouch Group plc
Printed by Scotprint

Fab friends

Think about your friendships with these fun activities!

Cool quiz
Find out your friendship type with this great quiz!

1. It's your birthday. Would you rather...

A. Invite a friend out for the day?

B. Go for a burger with a few mates?

C. Have a party and invite everyone you know?

2. What is the most fun at Brownies?

A. Doing an activity with a partner.

B. Getting together with your Six.

C. Playing a game with the whole Pack.

3. Your class is going on a trip. Who do you sit with on the coach?

A. You always sit with the same person.

B. There are a few people you're happy to sit with.

C. You don't mind – you'll chat to anyone!

4. You're away on a long holiday and miss your mates. Do you...

A. Write a long letter to that one special friend?

B. Send four or five postcards to the rest of your gang?

C. Send one postcard to your whole class at school?

5. You've just got a new pet rabbit. Do you...

A. Invite your friend over to play with it?

B. Tell your mates they can see it when they all come round?

C. Take a photo and show it to everybody you can think of?

Mostly A: One and only
You like to have one best friend who means the world to you! You are loyal to your best friend, and share everything with her.

Mostly B: In the gang
You're happiest as part of a small group of friends. You all get on well and have a lot of fun together.

Mostly C: Friend to all
You will find a friend everywhere you go! You're always ready to meet new people and make lots of new friends.

Super secret

These two best friends have their own secret code!
Can you crack it to find out what their messages say?

❀▲ ❋✛,❋▢● ❀✛■ ❋✛❋◆ ✛○◆❀ ▢❋❀◆❋ ◗❋✛√○▲◆❋?
❋✛○◆ ◆❋❋▢.

_ _ _, _?
_ _ _ _ _ _ _ _ .

▼◆▢❋ ◆❋❋▢, ▲ √✛■❋▼ ❋✛○◆ ❀✛ ❋✛❋◆ ✛○◆❋.
❖◆◆ ❀✛■ ❋▢○◆❋, ❋✛.

_ _ _ _ _ _ _ _ _ _, _ _ _ _ _ _ _ _ _ _ _ _ _ _ _ _ .
_ _ _ _ _ _ _ _ _ _ _ _ , _ _ .

▢	◗	❋	▼	◆	❀	❋	❀	▲	❀	❋	❋	●	✛	✛	❋	❖	❀	■	○	√	✛	❀	✏
A	B	C	D	E	F	G	H	I	J	K	L	M	N	O	P	Q	R	S	T	U	V	WX	Y Z

Look at page 76 for the answer!

Great mates

What is great about your friends? Pick five of these
words to describe what makes a really special friend.

Fun   Reliable   Sensible

Loyal   Giggly   Honest

Clever

Same interests   Lively

Cheerful

Sixer tip

Check out page 88 in
your *Brownies Adventure
On* book to find a great
friendship activity.

Flying jewels

Get in a flutter with butterflies – the most beautiful and colourful of insects.

Very hungry caterpillars

Butterflies begin their lives in eggs. These are usually laid on leaves by the adult butterfly. Different kinds of butterflies lay their eggs on certain plants. For example, the Red Admiral lays its eggs on nettles. Caterpillars hatch out of the eggs and eat the plant's leaves. In fact they hardly stop eating – some grow a hundred times heavier in just a few weeks!

Yves Lanceau/NHPA

All change

A caterpillar sheds its skin several times as it grows. When it is big enough, it finds a safe place to hide and sheds its skin for the last time. It makes a hard case around itself for protection. Now it is called a pupa or chrysalis. After a while the pupa splits open and a butterfly crawls out.

On the wing

At first the butterfly's wings are wet and crumpled. It needs to hang upside down and let the wings dry and stretch out. Then it can take off to look for food. Butterflies drink nectar, a sugary liquid, out of flowers. They have long, curled-up tongues which they can uncurl and put into flowers. The tongue is hollow, like a straw, so the butterfly can suck up nectar.

Colour coded

Butterflies' wings are covered with lots of tiny coloured scales. These make up the beautiful patterns we see. Bright colours attract other butterflies. They also scare off birds and other creatures that like to eat butterflies. However not all butterflies are brilliantly coloured. Some have brown or green wings that help them hide against trees and plants.

BADGE LINK

Wildlife explorer

Gardener

The garden gang

About 60 kinds of butterfly live in Britain, although more visit in the summer. If you have a garden you might see Large Whites, Small Whites, Red Admirals, Small Tortoiseshells or Peacocks. In the countryside you could spot Orange Tips, Common Blues or Small Coppers.

Fave flowers

Butterflies are becoming less common in Britain. You can help by growing plants that they like in your garden. You may not fancy planting nettles or thistles, but butterflies love them! Other favourites are lavender, marigolds and buddleia, which is also known as the 'butterfly bush'.

Flutterby facts

☆ Butterflies live all over the world, and there are about 28,000 different kinds of butterfly!

☆ The Monarch butterfly flies thousands of miles every year. It spends its summers in Canada and migrates to sunny Mexico in the winter.

☆ The largest butterfly in the world is the rare Queen Alexandra Birdwing butterfly. It lives in Papua New Guinea, a large island north of Australia. Its wings can be 30cm across!

☆ Most butterflies are not very speedy, but some skipper butterflies can fly at 30 miles an hour.

☆ Butterflies need to be warm to fly. If you see one perching in a sunny place, it might be sunbathing to get itself warm.

Turn the page to make a great butterfly belt!

Beautiful butterfly

You need

pencil ★ thin card ★ scissors ★ 3 pieces of felt in different colours ★ needle ★ cotton ★ pins ★ PVA glue ★ four 130cm lengths of ribbon, about 1cm wide, in different colours

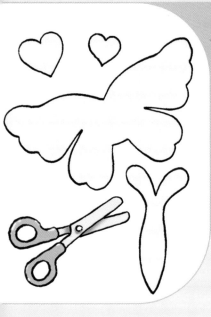

1

Draw a butterfly wings shape, a body shape and two hearts onto thin card. The wings should be about 12cm x 7cm. Cut them out. Now lay the wings template onto a piece of felt and draw round it twice. Cut out the wings.

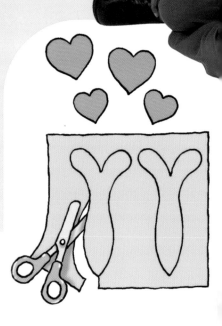

2

Place the heart templates onto the second piece of felt and draw round each one twice. Cut the hearts out. On the third piece of felt, draw round the body template twice and cut out.

3

Carefully place the hearts onto one of the wing pieces, with the bigger hearts at the top and the smaller ones at the bottom. Sew or glue the hearts onto the wings.

4 Stick or sew the two body shapes together. Stick or sew them onto the wing piece that you have just decorated with the hearts.

5 Cut out a piece of felt approximately 1.5cm by 2.5cm. Pin it onto the middle of the second wing piece to make a loop. Make sure the loop is big enough for the ribbons to fit through. Sew the loop at each end so it is firmly attached.

1.5cm

2.5cm

6 Pin the two wing pieces together, making sure the hearts and the loop are facing outwards. Sew or stick the pieces together.

7 Thread the ribbons through the loop on the back of your butterfly. To wear, wrap your belt around your waist and knot it at the side so the ribbons hang down.

BADGE LINK

Craft
GLUE

spring song

Illustrated by Sue Hagerty

On the grassy banks
Lambkins at their pranks;
Woolly sisters, woolly
brothers,
    Jumping off their feet,
While their woolly mothers
    Watch by them and bleat.

Christina Rossetti

Go global!

Take a spin around the world with these great international puzzles!

Wordsearch

Can you find all these countries in the grid?

Angola
Canada
Ecuador
Ghana
Iceland
Korea
Morocco
Oman
Poland
Sri Lanka
Uruguay
Wales

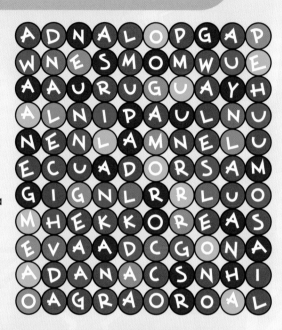

A D N A L O P G A P
W N E S M O M W U E
A A U R U G U A Y H
A L N I P A U L N U
N E N L A M N E L U
E C U A D O R S A M
G I G N L R R L U O
M H E K K O R E A S
E V A A D C G O N A
A D A N A C S N H I
O A G R A O R O A L

Flying the flag

Which of these flags are exactly alike?

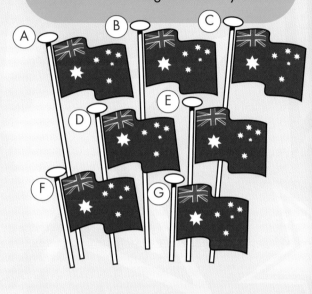

A B C D E F G

Animal planet

Match each animal to the continent where it lives.
Africa ★ Antarctica ★ Asia ★ Australasia ★
Europe ★ North America ★ South America

Crossed countries

See if you can fit all these country names in to the grid!
Chile ★ China ★ India ★ Iran ★ Italy ★
Japan ★ Kenya ★ Libya

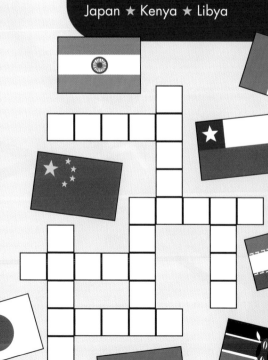

On holiday

All these lucky girls are going abroad on holiday.
Can you work out who is going to which country?
★ Canada ★ Egypt ★ Sweden ★ New Zealand

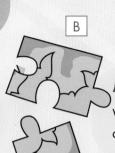
Ellie

'I'm going halfway round the world.'

'I'll need to take warm clothes.'

a

'I'll be able to visit the Great Pyramids.'

Jodi

rah

'I might see beavers, bears and moose.'

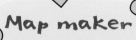

Map maker

Which piece will complete the map?

A
B
C
D
E
F

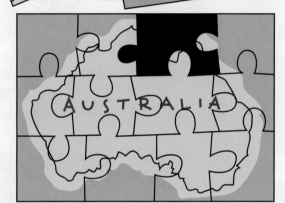

AUSTRALIA

Riddle me this

Solve this riddle to find the name of a country.

My first is in **coffee** but not in a **cake**,
My second's in **bread** but isn't in **bake**.
My third's in **potato** and also in **pea**,
My fourth is in **dinner** but never in **tea**.
My fifth is in **cherry** but isn't in **pear**,
My sixth is in **gâteau** and also **éclair**.
I'm the name of a country that's over the sea;
But you could catch a train to come and visit me!

What country am I? _ _ _ _ _ _

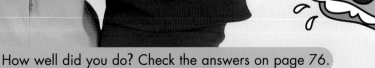

How well did you do? Check the answers on page 76.

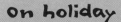

Brazil-liant!

Big, bold and beautiful, Brazil has something for everyone! Find out more abut this larger-than-life land.

Totally tropical

Brazil is a huge country – the biggest in South America and the fifth largest in the whole world. It's a great place if you like sunshine, as the weather is hot all year round. Brazil has bustling cities, vast rainforests, the mighty Amazon River and many miles of beautiful coast.

Jacques Jangoux/Science Photo Library

Fantastic football

Football is the national sport of Brazil, and is very popular. The Brazilian team is among the best in the world. Brazil has won the World Cup more times than any other country. It also boasts the largest stadium in the world, in the city of Rio de Janeiro. A hundred thousand people can cheer on their team in the massive Maracaña stadium.

Amazing Amazon

The huge Amazon River and the rainforests around it cover one third of Brazil. The river is over 4,000 miles long – the second longest in the world. It is home to many creatures including turtles and giant otters, dolphins, alligators and, of course, lots of fish!

Forest facts

The rainforests of Brazil are home to many thousands of animals, birds, insects and plants. They are also home to people. Some tribes of people live in the forest as they have done for hundreds of years. Sadly, vast areas of rainforest are being cut down to make room for farmland. The people of the forests are losing their homes, and wildlife such as the jaguar is in serious danger.

Getty Images

Party time!

Carnival is one of the most exciting festivals in Brazil. It is held in February or March and lasts four days. There are parades, music, dancing, fireworks and lots of parties. People come from all over the world to enjoy Carnival in Rio de Janeiro, where dancers parade through the streets in fabulous costumes and masks.

Food, glorious food

Some of our favourite foods are grown in Brazil, including tropical fruits like bananas, melons, pineapples, mangos and oranges. Coffee, chocolate and sugar are also important crops. Of course Brazil nuts come from this country too! The national dish of Brazil is *feijoada* (say it fezh-wah-da), a stew made from meat and beans.

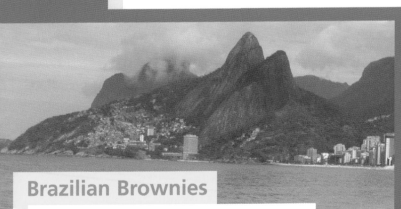

Brazilian Brownies

Brownies in Brazil are called Cirandas and are aged between six and nine. They are the youngest members of the guiding family. Cirandas wear blue and yellow uniforms. Brazilian Guides are called Bandeirantes.

Brazilian bites

Bombocado

These tasty coconut brownies are totally tropical!

Ingredients

3 eggs ★ 50g plain flour ★ 25g margarine ★ 1 tablespoon baking powder ★ 400ml milk ★ 350g sugar ★ 80g grated mozzarella cheese ★ 100g dessicated coconut ★ pinch of salt

You need

23cm square cake tin ★ greaseproof paper and a little margarine for greasing ★ blender ★ skewer ★ wire cooling tray ★ knife

1 Line the cake tin with greaseproof paper. Grease it lightly with margarine.

2 Put all the ingredients into a blender. Whizz until they are mixed well together. Pour the mixture into the greased cake tin.

Be safe

3 Put the oven on to 180°C/350°F/gas mark 4. Cook for about 1 hour 15 mins. Test the cake by pushing a skewer in; if it comes out sticky, the cake needs a little more cooking. Cool the cake on a wire cooling tray, then cut it into bars.

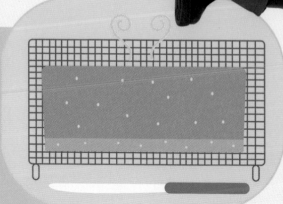

Illustrated by Claire Chrystall

Empadinhas

These little cheese pies are great in lunchboxes or on picnics!

Ingredients

For the crust:
45g butter ★ 250g plain fl`our ★ 1 egg yolk ★ 1 teaspoon salt ★ a little water

For the filling:
25g butter ★ 2 eggs ★ 225g cheese ★ 125ml milk

You need

saucepan ★ bowl ★ sieve ★ wooden spoon ★ 18 small muffin tins ★ whisk or fork ★ grater

1

Be safe

To make the crust, carefully melt the butter in a saucepan over a low heat. Pour it into the bowl. Sift in the flour and add the salt.

Separate the egg and mix in the yolk. Stir the mixture until it makes a firm ball. If it is crumbly, add a few drops of water at a time until it is firm enough.

2

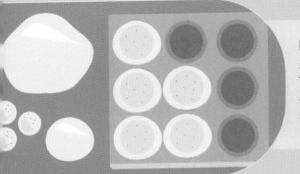

Pull off a small piece of the mixture, about the size of a golf ball. Roll it into a smooth ball. Then flatten it into a circle. Press it into a muffin tin so that it covers the bottom and sides. Line the rest of the muffin tins in the same way.

3

4

To make the filling, melt the butter in the saucepan over a low heat. Put the eggs in a bowl and beat them with a fork or whisk. Mix the butter in with the eggs. Grate the cheese and stir in. Add the milk and mix it in.

Be safe

Carefully spoon the mixture into the pasty-lined muffin tins. Cook at 180°C/ 350°F/gas mark 4 for 25 minutes, until your pies are golden-brown on top. Put them on a wire tray to cool.

5

Illustrated by Liz McIntosh

Talk to the animals

We all wish our pets could really speak to us! But even though they can't talk in words, they can often tell us how they are feeling. What's your animal friend trying to tell you?

 A dog's life

★ Everyone knows that a happy hound will wag its tail!

★ If dog is scared, it crouches down small, flattens its ears, tucks its tail in and may creep away.

★ When a pooch rolls over and shows its stomach, it's telling you it trusts you.

★ A dog that lifts its head and pricks up its ears is saying 'I want to play!'

 Rabbiting on

★ Thumping the back feet can be a danger sign.
It can also mean anger, or a bossy bunny asking for attention!

★ A really relaxed rabbit will stretch out on its stomach or side.

★ Nervous bunnies will crouch down small with their ears pressed down flat.

★ A rabbit that rubs its chin on you is marking you with its scent, because it thinks you are important.

 **Cat chat**

★ If a kitty sitting on your lap kneads you with its paws, it is feeling happy.

★ Angry cats fluff up their fur to look bigger, twitch their tails, get their claws out ready to fight, hiss and spit.

★ A moggy that is pleased to see you holds its tail straight up, with its ears pointing forwards.

★ A purring cat is, of course, very contented!

Guinea pig gossip

★ If you stop stroking your guinea pig, a nudge with the nose means 'Please carry on'.
★ A bright, happy young guinea will do wiggly jumps in the air!
★ If your guinea pig feels aggressive it will fluff its fur and stand up tall, showing its teeth.
★ A guinea that stalks like a cat, swaying its back end from side to side, is showing who is boss.

Hamster habits

★ A cross hamster will click its teeth at you.
★ If your hamster sits down for a wash, it is feeling safe and secure.
★ A nervous hammy will creep along low to the floor with its ears pressed down flat.
★ Hamsters ask 'What's going on?' by standing up on their back legs and pricking their ears.

Registered Charity no 219099

Calling all animal lovers!

Do you love animals? Well so does the RSPCA, and we have 100 fantastic RSPCA Animal Action Club memberships to give away!

The lucky winners will receive a great pack full of information on animals, puzzles and quizzes! They will also get a copy of *Animal Action*, the RSPCA's magazine crammed full of animal news, posters, competitions, celebrity features and games. As an Animal Action Club member you will get six issues throughout the year.

To enter, answer this simple question: What does RSPCA stand for? Send your answer on a postcard, with your name, date of birth and address, to: RSPCA Animal Action Club (Brownie), Wilberforce Way, Southwater, Horsham, West Sussex RH13 9RS. The closing date for entries is 18th February 2005.

Data Protection Act: Winner information will be held on computer and will only be used by the RSPCA.

World of colour

There is more to colour than meets the eye!

What colour is light?

If you switch on an ordinary light bulb, you see white light. However light is actually made up of seven different colours. When they are mixed together you see white light. When they are separated you see all seven: red, orange, yellow, green, blue, indigo and violet. A rainbow is an example of light being separated into its different colours.

Peter Menzel/Science Photo Library

Why is an orange orange?

When you see objects that are different colours, what you are really seeing is light reflected off them. When white light hits an orange, all the colours in the light are absorbed (soaked up) except orange. The orange light bounces back and that is what our eyes see.

How many colours are there?

Make a list of all the colours can you think of. How many could you name? Now would you be surprised to learn that humans can see about seven million different colours? We can see different shades of colour, for example light greens, dark greens. We can also see different hues of a colour, like bluey-greens and yellowy-greens.

Can colour change how we feel?

Most colours can be divided into 'warm' and 'cool' colours. Warm colours are reds, oranges and yellows. Think of the sun, fire or hot deserts. Cool colours are greens and blues. They remind us of water, leaves and the sky. Warm colours will make you feel lively. Cool colours help you to feel relaxed and calm.

How are colours made?

Today, artificial colours like paints and dyes are made from chemicals. In the days before chemicals, people made colours from natural materials. For example, browns and oranges were made from earth. Greens and yellows came from different plants. A certain kind of shellfish gave purple dye, and deep red was made by crushing beetles!

Do animals see colour?

Most animals do not see colours in the same way that humans do. Some animals, such as birds, butterflies and bees, can see many more colours than people can. Dogs cannot tell the difference between reds, oranges, yellows and greens, but they see more shades of blue and purple than people can.

⭐ Try this

⭐ Find out how coloured inks are made from a mixture of different colours. You will need a glass with a little water in, a piece of kitchen roll and some felt pens.

⭐ Draw some blobs of colour near the bottom of the piece of kitchen roll. (Black and brown are good colours to try.) Now stand the piece of kitchen roll in the glass of water. Watch what happens as the water creeps up the paper!

Turn to page 76 to find out why this happens!

Understanding how to use colour will help you create great art. Have a go at this activity and really get to grips with colour!

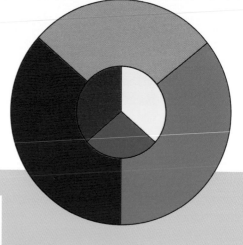

Mix and match

Mix and match

You need

tracing paper ★ pencil ★ white paper ★ old newspaper ★ apron ★ red, yellow, blue, black and white poster paints ★ paintbrushes ★ old saucer for mixing paint

1

Start by drawing a simple picture or design on the tracing paper. Don't make it too small or it will be difficult to paint! Flowers or butterflies are good things to draw. Now trace the picture onto five pieces of white paper.

2

Spread out some newspaper to protect your painting area. Put on an apron to keep your clothes clean. For your first painting, use *primary* colours. These are three colours that you cannot make by mixing other colours. They are red, yellow and blue. They are found at the centre of the colour wheel. Paint your first picture using just these three colours.

Blue

Red

Yellow

Illustrated by Stuart Lynch

3 On the outside ring of the colour wheel are the *secondary* colours: green, orange and purple. They are made by mixing two primary colours: red and yellow = orange, red and blue = purple, yellow and blue = green. Mix your paints to make secondary colours and use them to paint your second picture.

4 Colours that are opposite each other on the colour wheel are called *complementary* colours. Blue and orange, yellow and purple, red and green are pairs of complementary colours. Choose one pair and use them to paint your third picture.

5 The lightness or darkness of a colour is called the *tone*. Pick one colour, such as blue, and mix several different tones by adding different amounts of white. The more white you add, the lighter tones you will get. Do not add any other colours. Paint your fourth picture using just these tones.

6 *Harmonic* colours are groups of colours that are near each other on the colour wheel. For example, red, orange and yellow would be a group of harmonic colours. Red, purple and blue are another group. Choose a group of harmonic colours and paint your last picture with these.

Take a look at your finished pictures. Which one looks best? Which one is the brightest? Which colours look really good together? Which ones look horrible? Keep your pictures with your painting things. Next time you do some painting they will help you to choose beautiful colours.

Dad came home from work the other week with his old office computer carefully resting on the back seat of his car.

'Got into work this morning to find that my boss had upgraded all the computers in the place.'

'But I can't see much wrong with this one – it's just got a little scratch on it,' I said.

'Ah,' said Dad, 'but the memory is almost used up, and all the new technology means that programmes are better and work quicker too. Most companies and organisations need to upgrade their computers every three or four years anyway. Of course, as senior salesman for Doggydos Biscuits I need to remain at the cutting edge of today's technology!'

'So what are you going to do with that one, Dad?' I asked.

'I'll take it to the tip in the morning,' he said.

It seemed a bit of a waste to me but I said I'd go with him so I could get out of tidying my bedroom. Cool!

The next morning we arrived at our local 'civic amenities site' (why can't they just call it a dump like everyone else?). Dad struggled up the metal stairs to the first enormous skip carrying the screen and control box, and I stumbled along behind with the keyboard and mouse. Why had Dad left them all still connected to each other? When Dad reached the top of the steps he put it all on the edge of the skip. He was just going to push it all over when there was a great:

'Stoooooooopppppp!!!'

But Dad was still holding all the old computer stuff, and the yell made him jump so he dropped it! He disappeared over the side and that dragged the keyboard in too. I was left standing on the steps holding the computer mouse like a precious toy! Luckily for Dad, the skip had been almost full, so he hadn't fallen very far. He was sitting on a mound of black sacks with the computer on his lap.

'Caught it,' said Dad. The caretaker who looks after the dump came running up the stairs in a panic. He was scared in case Dad had hurt himself.

He helped Dad get out and we went to his office, where he gave Dad a mug of tea. He told us he'd just heard about a recycling project for computers, which he was keen to explore. He said that nearly a MILLION TONNES of electrical and electronic stuff was being thrown away every year, and a lot of this was computers and all the bits that go with them. That's an awful lot of electrical rubbish!

'But what can be done with it?' asked Dad. 'After all, we're getting rid of it because it's overloaded and out of date.'

'There are organisations around who train unemployed people to do up old computers and upgrade the systems. These people are then often able to find jobs using their new skills, and the refurbished computers are donated to good causes: schools, charities, disabled people and those who don't earn very much. Some of them are sent to other countries through charities. If it's OK with you, I'll pass your PC on to one of these organisations.'

'Of course,' said Dad. Well, this sounded a much better idea to me than just sending it all to machine heaven.

'We wanted to get an old computer for Brownies, ' I said to Dad, 'so that we could check out all the Brownie news on the Girlguiding UK website from time to time, and make posters and write letters. Do you think they might have a spare one?'

'I'll have a word and let your dad know,' said the caretaker, taking down Dad's telephone number.

A couple of weeks later, Dad arrived in the middle of Brownies carrying a gleaming white computer.

'A present from the computer recycling project,' he announced. 'Perhaps Dot can tell you all about it while I set this up for you.'

'... So, you see, an old computer need not be rubbish,' I said when I'd finished my talk, pointing to our brand new computer. But as I pointed at it, my eye caught sight of... could it really be... a familiar little scratch!

After the computer episode, I decided to find out a bit more about recycling. There's more to it than just putting jam jars in a bottle bank! Did you know that about three quarters of the 'rubbish' we throw away could actually be recycled?
Why not check out your 'green' knowledge by having a go at this quiz?
You'll find the answers on page 76.

Circle time

Circle all the things that can be recycled.
glass paper newspaper clothes drinks cans plastic bottles shoes computers

Go green

Fill in the missing words to find some good green ideas!

water   trees

cycle   birds   light

Switch off the _ _ _ _ _ when you leave the room.
Save _ _ _ _ _ – buy recycled paper.
Walk or _ _ _ _ _ on short journeys – don't go in the car.
Help _ _ _ _ _ by feeding them in winter.
Save _ _ _ _ _ – turn off dripping taps.

True or false?

Which of these recycling statements are true?
a. Each household in the UK produces about one tonne of rubbish every year.
b. In Britain, we recycle more than in any other countries.
c. There are over 20,000 bottle banks in Britain.
d. One third of all household 'rubbish' is kitchen and garden waste.
e. You can't recycle mobile phones.
f. Taking a shower uses half as much water as having a bath.
g. You can put kitchen foil in can banks.

Find out more about Dot's adventures – visit her at her very own web site
www.missdorothy.com

Web safe

Creature

Go wild with these fun puzzles on a wildlife theme!

Who am I?

Join the dots to find an animal!

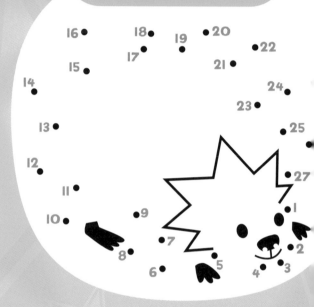

Looks a bit fishy!

How many fish are in the pond?

Wild wordsearch

Can you find all these wildlife words in the grid?

Newt
Porpoise
Toad
Starfish
Dormouse
Shrew
Falcon
Robin
Spider
Ladybird

S	E	D	S	N	R	F	L	D	D	S
T	E	S	E	M	R	O	D	R	E	H
S	C	W	U	D	T	H	B	R	S	R
I	T	E	P	O	R	P	O	I	S	E
I	A	D	A	N	M	E	F	N	N	W
L	A	D	Y	B	I	R	D	N	L	R
I	R	R	D	S	A	O	O	I	L	E
P	O	D	T	T	A	C	S	D	P	B
R	B	S	S	S	L	D	D	O	O	S
I	S	O	N	A	I	A	W	D	I	O
S	O	I	F	H	W	P	W	O	R	S

Illustrated by Andi Good

feature

Home sweet home

Follow the tunnels to find out which rabbit lives in which burrow.

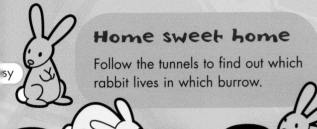

Mopsy

Topsy

A   B   C

Long story

How many animal names can you find on the centipede?

EMDFROGOSYDEERALMOTHETAWRATOCHIMOLENITOADEGOWLAR

Dinner time!

Can you spot eight differences between these two pictures?

How well did you do? Check the answers on page 77.

Magic beans!

When was the last time you ate some chocolate? Probably not so long ago! Now you can find out just where your sweet treat came from.

Top trees

Did you know that chocolate grows on trees? The cacao tree grows in hot, rainy places like West Africa and South America. 'Cacao' meant 'god food' in Mayan, an ancient language. The Maya people lived in South America and worshipped the cacao tree.

Full of beans

Cocoa pods, which look like yellow rugby balls, grow on the trees. They are filled with cocoa beans. Farmers cut the ripe pods from the trees and carefully take out the beans. Next the cocoa beans are spread out in the sun to dry. The farmers then sort the beans and pack them into sacks for transport to a factory.

Mass produced

At the factory, the beans need to be roasted in ovens. Roasting gives them a deeper brown colour and a more chocolatey flavour. Next they are ground up to make a thick liquid called cocoa mass. But this still isn't chocolate as we know it! To make chocolate, cocoa mass has to be mixed with other ingredients, such as sugar and milk.

Chocolate money

People have enjoyed chocolate for many hundreds of years. However the Maya people did not eat chocolate – they drank it. Their chocolate drink was not like our cocoa; it was bitter and spicy. It was drunk only by rich people and at religious ceremonies. In those days cocoa beans were very precious, and were even used as money!

Chocolate spreads

The Spanish first brought chocolate to Europe, in the 16th century. They made a sweet chocolate drink with sugar and vanilla, and it soon became popular all over Europe. The first chocolate bar was made in England in 1847. Since then chocolate has grown more and more popular. In the UK we now eat over half a million tons of it every year.

Fair food

Life can be very hard for a cacao farmer. Many farmers are not paid enough for the cocoa beans they produce. An organisation that makes sure farmers are fairly paid is the Fairtrade Foundation. When you buy chocolate or cocoa with the FAIRTRADE Mark on it, you can be sure that the farmers who grew it have been paid a fair price for their cocoa beans.

Sixer tip

Why not have a Fairtrade evening at Brownies? You could make yummy Fairtrade chocolate treats and serve Fairtrade fruit juice.

FAIRTRADE | Guarantees a **better deal** for Third World Producers ®

Look for this Mark on Fairtrade products

Fairtrade facts

☆ Fairtrade is not just about chocolate. You can also buy Fairtrade tea, coffee, fruit juices, bananas, biscuits and snacks.

☆ Fairtrade helps 500,000 farmers and workers to earn a fair price and have better working conditions.

☆ For more information, have a look at the Fairtrade web site at www.fairtrade.org.uk

Web safe

BADGE LINK

World issues

Chocs away!

Satisfy a sweet tooth with these delicious chocolate dishes.

Choc-orange bites

Try these yummy chocolate nibbles for an extra-special treat!

Illustrated by Beccy Blake

Ingredients

150g Fairtrade dark chocolate ★ 2 tablespoons golden syrup ★ 2 tablespoons cocoa powder ★ 100g butter ★ grated zest of 1 large orange ★ 225g digestive biscuits

You need

saucepan ★ wooden spoon ★ freezer bag ★ rolling pin ★ grater ★ plate ★ petit four cases

1 Put the chocolate, golden syrup, cocoa powder and butter in a saucepan. Stir them gently over a low heat until they have melted together.

Be safe

2 Put the digestive biscuits into a freezer bag and crush them with a rolling pin.

3 Stir the crushed biscuits and orange zest into the melted chocolate mixture. Leave the mixture until it is cool enough to touch.

4 Using the palms of your hands, roll the mixture into small balls. Put the balls on a plate and pop them into the fridge to set for about 30 minutes. Once the balls have set, make them look extra special by putting each ball into a petit four case.

Hot chocolate

What could be nicer than a mug of hot choc on a cool day?

Ingredients

50g cocoa powder ★ 30g sugar ★ 60ml water ★ small pinch of salt ★ ½ teaspoon vanilla extract ★ 500ml milk ★ toppings such as grated chocolate, squirty cream or mini marshmallows

You need

small saucepan ★ wooden spoon ★ 2 mugs

1 Put the cocoa and sugar into the saucepan. Mix them well together.

BADGE LINK

Cook

Cook

2 **Be safe**

Turn the heat onto a low setting. Add the water a little bit at a time. Stir all the time until you have made a smooth syrup.

3 Add the salt and vanilla extract and mix well.

5 Carefully pour the hot chocolate into mugs. For an extra touch, serve with squirty cream, grated chocolate or some mini marshmallows on the top.

4 Add the milk and stir until heated. Be careful not to let the mixture boil.

The Grand Raffle

Rita couldn't concentrate. She was really excited, because tonight after Brownies she was going to Great-Granny-Violet's house. She looked forward to these visits because Granny always made hot apple pie and told amazing stories about her life.

'Today I thought we could talk about ways to raise money for our Brownie holiday'

Brown Owl interrupted Rita's thoughts. 'Today I thought we could talk about ways to raise money for our Brownie holiday. Does anyone have any ideas?'

Rita's Pack was made up of four very different Sixes, who liked to do very different things. Each Six always worked separately within the Pack, however hard Brown Owl tried to get them to work together.

At first all the girls sat quietly thinking, then Abigail, the Sixer of the Foxes, spoke up. 'We could put on a play, or a talent contest – starring the Foxes!' The Foxes were very confident. They always talked the most in Pow-wows but sometimes they got told off by Brown Owl for being too noisy!

'That's a good idea,' said Brown Owl, 'but we need to do something that includes the whole Pack. How many of you would like to do a play?' Only the Foxes raised their hands.

'I know,' said Sam. 'We could make things and sell them to raise money.' Sam was one of the Rabbits, the artistic members of the Pack, who were really good at painting and crafts. Brown Owl put the idea to the vote, and again, the Rabbits were the only ones who wanted to do what they'd suggested.

The Squirrels were known for being really good at maths. At Brownies they liked playing games that

involved quick thinking, and they always volunteered to collect and count the subs at each meeting. Natasha, one of the Squirrels, suggested they hold a sponsored swim and that they look after all the money raised. As before, though, only the Squirrels thought this was a good idea.

'What about you, Rita, you're usually full of good ideas. How do you think we should raise money for the holiday?' asked Brown Owl.

'Um… er,' said Rita, who had been thinking about hot apple pie.

Rita was the Sixer of the Badgers. Her Six was very good at organising things and liked to help Brown Owl plan the meetings, but this week they were being very quiet.

'Well, we've got some ideas to be going on with,' said Brown Owl. 'Think about it during the week, and we'll make a decision at our next meeting.'

Great-Granny-Violet was so old that she had been Rita's age during the Second World War. She claimed that she was over a hundred years old but Rita's mum said she was more like 75, although even she couldn't be sure.

'When I was in the Brownies, our uniforms came down to our ankles'

When they were sitting at the kitchen table eating apple pie, Rita told Granny about what had happened at Brownies that night. 'Ah, you have such lovely, colourful uniforms now,' sighed Granny. 'When I was in the Brownies, our uniforms came down to our ankles and we had to wear helmets because our meeting place was falling down.' She raised one grey eyebrow mischievously. Rita could never be sure about whether Granny was exaggerating or not, but this sounded like the beginning of a story so she didn't question her.

'In fact,' said Granny, 'during the war a bomb fell very close to our hut and we had to find somewhere else to meet. Luckily a local farmer had an outhouse that he said we could use. It was very run-down and cold, and we still had to wear our helmets because chickens had taken to roosting in the rafters!'

Rita giggled.

'As if that wasn't enough, another Brownie Pack used the outhouse on the same night. As you can imagine, the conditions were very cramped and the other Pack started to accuse us of copying their ideas!

'To stop us arguing, our Brown Owl suggested that we all sit down together and work out how to make the hall more comfortable. Now, this didn't seem like a good idea at all, but then one of the Brownies from the other Pack said that her uncle was a roofer, who might be able to patch up the roof. Hilda's mum offered to repair the curtains from our old hut. My dad, your great-great-grandfather, was a painter, and he offered to help us paint the hall.

'Soon, the whole town was involved. In a couple of weeks, we had brand-new windows, freshly painted walls, a new wooden floor and lovely clean curtains. Best of all, the other Pack joined us and we had a bigger and better Brownie Pack than ever before!'

On the way home Rita and her mum passed a tree with a poster attached to it. It was advertising the Twinning summer fête, which was to be held next Saturday on the village green. Rita had an idea.

Next week at Brownies, Brown Owl started the Pow-wow in the same way.

'Do any of you have any more ideas about how to raise money for our Brownie holiday?'

This time Rita spoke up straight away. 'Look at this,' she said and passed around a poster for the fête. 'I think we should have a raffle. The Foxes are good at talking to people – they could go around the shops in Twinning with Brown Owl, asking for things to offer as prizes. The Rabbits can decorate the stall; the Squirrels can look after all the money we make; and the Badgers can help Brown Owl to organise it all and run it on the day.'

Brown Owl smiled. 'That's a very good idea Rita, and it includes everyone – who thinks we should hold a raffle?'

This time everyone raised their hands and there was lots of excited chattering. The girls set to work.

On Saturday morning the Pack met on the village green before the fête began. A bouncy castle was

being blown up and lots of people were setting up stalls. The Squirrels were helping the Rabbits to put a banner up above the stall. The Rabbits had made it earlier in the week, with the words 'The Grand Raffle' painted in big colourful letters along its length.

'We got lots of goodies,' said Abigail, who had gone to all the shops with the Foxes and Brown Owl that morning, to ask for prizes. 'All the shopkeepers were really kind. The only one who didn't want to give us anything was Mr Pickles from the sweet shop. But I told him that it would be a good advert for his shop and he gave us this!' She reached into a big blue sack and pulled out a gold box of chocolates, tied with a blue ribbon.

Just then Granny walked across the grass, struggling under the weight of a huge cardboard box. It was full of apple pies to sell at the fête. 'You did well to get anything from him,' she said. 'I went to Twinning School with Edward Pickles and he was always mean, even then. His parents owned the sweet shop and he used to come to school with his pockets full of sweets. How we longed for a gobstopper or a pineapple cube — but he kept them all to himself!'

As Granny set up her stall, the Foxes emptied the box of prizes onto the grass. The girls gathered around. There was a big fluffy teddy bear from the toy-shop; a voucher from the hairdressers; a bright green bottle of bubble bath from the chemist; a book and an S Club 8 CD from the book shop and lots of food from the greengrocers.

'What do you think should be the first prize?' Brown Owl asked.

'It should be the S Club CD,' said Abigail. 'They're the best!'

'Or the book – it's got a really pretty cover,' said Sam.

Suddenly everyone started speaking at once, offering suggestions for what the first prize should be.

Everyone started speaking at once, offering suggestions for what the first prize should be

Brown Owl couldn't even hear herself think. She was just about to suggest that they put the idea to a vote, when Rita said, 'The first prize should be the thing that's worth the most money. The Squirrels are good with money – they should make the decision.'

The girls quietened down and Natasha spoke. 'I think it's probably the box of chocolates. That looks very expensive.'

'The box of chocolates it is!' said Rita and put it in the middle of the raffle table.

The Brownies set about attaching tickets to the prizes and putting them out on the table. It soon became clear that, with all the prizes the Foxes had collected, there wasn't going to be enough room to display everything.

All the Brownies had different ideas about how to solve the problem. There was a real commotion as some started squashing prizes up on the table, and others started taking them away.

Again, Brown Owl thought that she would have to say something, but once again one of the Brownies spoke up.

'I know,' said Abigail. 'The Rabbits should decide. They're the best at making things look good.'

Sam went over to the box that had contained the apple pies and turned it upside down. 'Here's our extra table – all it needs is something to cover it. She picked up the sack that had contained all the prizes. 'Perfect!'

Brown Owl smiled.

That afternoon the raffle was a big success and everyone in the village was buying tickets. Rita looked around and saw Granny talking to some of the Brownies.

'I held a raffle once, you know, to help with the war effort. I gave away my pet iguana as the first prize.'

The Brownies looked at Granny in awe. Rita giggled to herself. She knew that Granny had never had a pet iguana!

She looked over at the Foxes who were selling tickets, and then at the stall. It looked brilliant, with a big colourful sign and two tables, which were slowly emptying as people bought more and more tickets. The Squirrels were busily counting money and the Badgers were doing a bit of everything.

Granny stood behind Rita and put her arm around her shoulders. 'See what you can do when you work together. I've saved some apple pies for you – you can share them when you've finished.'

'See what you can do when you work together'

Just then, Mr Pickles came up and bought a ticket. He was a little man with small wire-framed glasses and a very serious face. He looked at the number on his ticket and then searched for his prize. When he stopped in front of the box of chocolates his mouth stretched into a mean little smile.

'Well, I never,' said Granny. 'I don't think I've ever seen him smile before!'

When the stall had been packed away, the Squirrels did a final count of all the money and announced that the Pack had made over £100 for their holiday! With that, the 4th Twinning Brownies sat down on the grass together, eating apple pies and talking happily about their day.

Kate Fenning

Take the plunge

Next time you're bored on a rainy afternoon, why not ask to go swimming? You don't need to be a great swimmer to have a brilliant time at the pool.

Dive in!

One of the best things about swimming is that anyone can do it! There are lots of swimming pools all over the country. Many of them run swimming clubs for people of all abilities. Another good thing is that you don't need expensive equipment. Just a swimming costume and a towel will start you off.

Watery work-out

Swimming is not only fun – it's also really good exercise. You use lots of different muscles, so your whole body gets a great work-out. It makes you strong, because it takes an effort to push your body through water. Swimming helps keep your heart and lungs healthy too.

Down under

Once you can swim, a watery world is your oyster! You could learn snorkelling or scuba diving, and explore underwater. A snorkel lets you see and breathe while swimming under the surface. With scuba diving gear you can dive deeper. It's a great way to see some amazing wildlife. Some divers even find shipwrecks and sunken treasure!

AFP/Getty Images

Go for goals

If you like team sports, what about water polo, a ball game played in the pool? There are seven players in a water polo team. The aim is to score goals in nets which are placed at each end of the pool. Players swim around without touching the bottom, passing the ball to each other and shooting goals.

Move to the music

Getty Images

Why not try synchronised swimming, in which you do dance-like movements to music? You can work on your own, with a partner or in groups of 4–8 people. Synchronised swimmers have to be really fit, strong and graceful. If you love swimming, gymnastics and dance this could be a perfect sport for you!

To the rescue

If you and your friends are into swimming, it's a really good idea to learn lifesaving. You could be able to help anyone who gets into difficulties in the water. If you join a lifesaving scheme you can work for badges and certificates. There are even lifesaving competitions you could take part in.

BADGE LINK

Swimmer

Swimmer

Water safety

Watersports

Find out more

★ Ask about watery activities at your local pool. ★ For more on swimming, synchronised swimming and water polo, visit www.britishswimming.org.uk. ★ To find out about lifesaving, visit the Royal Life Saving Society's web site at www.rlss.org.uk. ★ The British Sub-Aqua Club has a great snorkelling site at www.bsacsnorkelling.co.uk. ★ Learn more about scuba diving at www.padi.com.

Web safe

Royal life

Have you ever thought about growing up and marrying a prince? The President of Girlguiding UK, Her Royal Highness The Countess of Wessex, did just that. Read on to find out all about her life and work.

Early years

When she was young, Sophie Rhys-Jones was a keen Brownie! She also enjoyed lots of different sports. She was in her school's netball, hockey, athletics, gymnastics and swimming teams. Some of her other hobbies were ballet and acting.

At work

After she left college, Sophie Rhys-Jones worked in public relations. Public relations means helping people to understand what companies or organisations do. She worked for different companies including a radio station. In 1996 she set up her own company, which she ran for five years.

Royal wedding

Sophie Rhys-Jones met Prince Edward at a charity tennis event in 1993. Six years later, the couple got engaged. They were married in the chapel at Windsor Castle, one of the Queen's homes, in June 1999. Thousands of people lined the streets as the newly married couple drove past in a horse-drawn carriage.

PA Photos/John Stillwell

Family life

When they got married, the Queen gave Prince Edward the title Earl of Wessex and his wife became Countess of Wessex. In 2003 they had a baby daughter, named Lady Louise Mountbatten-Windsor. The family lives at a big country house in Surrey.

PA Photos/Johnny Green

PA Photos/Andrew Parsons

Our President

In June 2003 the Countess became Girlguiding UK's new President. As President she has official duties, such as presenting awards. The Countess will also visit Girlguiding UK members and see some of the fun things Brownies, Guides, Rainbows and the Senior Section get up to!

Charity work

The Countess works for many different charities. Lots of these are children's charities, such as Sick Children in Wales and the Royal School for Deaf Children. She is also the Patron of the Central School of Ballet and of Sunderland Football Club's official charity. The Countess also travels to different countries with The Earl of Wessex to support his work.

PA Photos

These little salt dough characters are so easy to make – then you can use them to tell your favourite tales!

Fairytale fun

You need

100g plain flour ★ 100g salt ★ 1 teaspoon vegetable oil ★ 75ml water ★ bowl ★ spoon ★ old newspaper ★ apron ★ wire cooling tray ★ poster paints and brushes

1 Put the flour, salt, oil and water into a bowl. Mix it all together with your hands until you have a smooth dough.

2 Spread old newspaper over your table and put on an apron to protect your clothes. To make a princess, take a piece of dough about the size of a ping-pong ball. Break this piece in half. Roll one half with your hands to make a cone shape with flat ends. This makes the skirt.

3 Now take a piece of dough the size of a small marble. Roll it into a drum shape. Press it onto the top of the skirt. This makes the body.

Illustrated by Mary Hall

4 For the arms, take a small piece of dough and roll it into a long thin sausage. Place it on top of the body and press down flat in the middle. Move the arms into position. If they look too long, pinch off the ends. If they look too short, carefully squeeze them to make them longer and thinner.

5 Roll a piece of dough the size of a small marble. Press it on top of the figure to make the head. Make hair by rolling long, very thin strips of dough and pressing them onto the head. It may look a bit messy at the front, but you can cover this by shaping a little tiara or crown.

6 To make a prince, again take a piece of dough the size of a ping-pong ball. Break it in half. Instead of making one cone shape, break the piece of dough in half again and make two tall thin cones. Press them together for legs. Make the rest of the figure in the same way as the princess - but with shorter hair!

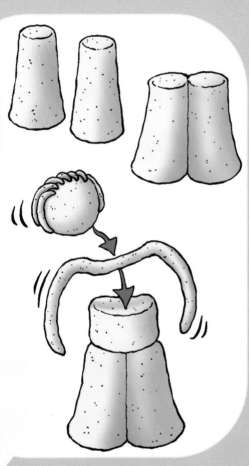

7 Now you know how the figures are made, you can create many other characters. You could make a king and queen, a witch or wizard, a fairy godmother, a best friend or sister for your princess. Use your imagination to try and make them all a bit different - taller or shorter, fatter or thinner, different hairstyles.

8 When you have finished, stand all your figures on a wire tray and leave them overnight to dry. The next day, paint them carefully. Once the paint is dry you can start to use your characters in stories!

Competition

Get creative and you could win a fantastic prize!

Have you ever tried delicious Brownies for Brownies or Biscuits for Brownies? If you've never seen these yummy cake mixes, have a look next time you're in your local supermarket. They're easy and fun to make, and you can decorate them however you like! Best of all, they are designed especially for Brownies!

Win! Win! Win!

Girlguiding UK has teamed up with Victoria Foods for this fab competition. Wouldn't you love to win one of these exciting prizes?

1st prize

The lucky winner will win a trip for herself and five Brownie friends to the factory where Brownies for Brownies and Biscuits for Brownies are made. You'll find out how the cake mixes are made and see the people and machines at work! You'll also get to have fun decorating some cakes yourselves and enjoy a tea party with plenty of treats! As if this wasn't enough, the winner will also take home a fantastic Brownie rucksack stuffed with goodies!

Runner-up prizes

Five runners-up will each win a selection of tasty cake mixes. Why not have a cookery evening at Brownies – you could sell your cakes to raise money, or just eat them all yourselves!

To win one of these great prizes, put your thinking cap on and dream up a design for a new Brownie cake. You can be as wild and wacky as you like – perhaps you'd love a pizza-flavoured cake, or one that only uses yellow ingredients! Send us a picture of your cake and a list of the ingredients you would put in it.

On the back of your entry, write:
- your name
- your age
- your address
- your Brownie Pack
- the three best things in your Brownie Annual
- the best thing about being a Brownie

Send your entry to:
Brownie Annual 2005
Victoria Foods Competition
Girlguiding UK
17-19 Buckingham Palace Road
London SW1W 0PT

The closing date for the competition is 18th February 2005.

The winning entry will be selected by Victoria Foods and Girlguiding UK. The judges' decision is final and no correspondence will be entered into. The first prize consists of a visit for 6 Brownies and 2 adults to the Victoria Foods factory in Leigh, Lancashire (transport not included), and a Brownie rucksack containing Brownie products from Girlguiding UK Trading Service. The runner-up prizes consist of boxes of assorted cake mixes.

Brownie brain

Brownies are busy people – so get busy with these fun puzzles!

Sweet treats

Can you spot eight differences between these two pictures?

Puppy puzzler!

These pups are so excited about going for a country walk, they have tangled up their leads! Can you work out which dog belongs to which girl?

Top of the shops

Lisa offered to do her gran's shopping, but she is in a bit of a muddle! Can you help her work out what to buy?

Emma

Rosie

Carrie

Daisy

Chester

Snowy

RANGOSE _ _ _ _ _ _ _
ERIC _ _ _ _
ATOOMEST _ _ _ _ _ _ _ _
TROUGHY _ _ _ _ _ _ _
STUCIBIS _ _ _ _ _ _ _ _
PETHIGATS _ _ _ _ _ _ _ _ _

Illustrated by Nick Diggory

teasers

Cross out all the letters that appear more then once. Rearrange the ones that are left over to find something that is important to Brownies.

A L O G B
S A T D U
M F B D K
G I D T E
K U R L F

_ _ _ _ _ _ _

odd sock?

Kim needs to pair up her socks and put them away. Help her match the pairs. Is there an odd sock left over?

Helping hand

Bethan is taking a letter to the post box. Can you help her find it?

Now take a look at the answers on page 77.

Mini mouse

With their little furry ears and bright eyes, harvest mice are not just Britain's smallest rodents – they're probably the cutest too!

Very, very tiny!

These tiny creatures are only 5–7cm long, about half the length of a pencil. They weigh about the same as a twenty-pence piece. Being so small and light, they can climb around in thick grass without ever touching the ground. They can even swim.

Neat nests

Harvest mice aren't just cute; they are also clever little animals. They weave round nests out of grass, high above the ground. The high nests keep them safe from foxes and other dangers. Mice line their nests with fluff to keep themselves and their babies warm.

Laurie Cambell / NHPA

Beautiful babies

Mouse mums can have two or three lots of babies in a year. There are usually about six babies in a litter. Although they are very tiny and helpless when they are born, harvest mice grow up fast. When they are just 11 weeks old they are ready to look after themselves.

Joe Blossom / NHPA

New houses

Harvest mice live in hedgerows and in fields of tall grass or reeds. Sadly these habitats have been destroyed to make room for more farming. The harvest mice have been left with fewer places to live. People have started to help by planting more hedgerows and even giving the mice old tennis balls, which are just the right size for a cosy nest!

Joe Blossom/NHPA

Monkey tails

Harvest mice are the only British mice with tails that can be used for climbing, just like monkeys! This leaves their front paws free for nest-building and for feeding. Seeds, grains and berries are a harvest mouse's favourite snacks. They will also eat roots, moss and occasional small insects.

Danger mouse

It's not easy to see a harvest mouse. They come out in daytime and at night, but are most active at dusk. They do not see very well, but luckily they have very sharp ears and can listen out for danger. The tiny mice are a favourite food for lots of other animals, such as foxes, weasels, owls and hawks.

Stephen Dalton/NHPA

Many mice

They may be the smallest, but harvest mice are not the only mice to live in Britain. The **wood mouse** lives in a small burrow which it digs in soft soil. The **hazel dormouse** has a thick, furry tail and sleeps through the winter in a round nest. The most common mouse is the **house mouse**, which likes to live near people.

Food glorious food

If you thought healthy food was boring, just wait till you try these scrumptious recipes!

Breaded burgers

With a crunchy coating and cheesy centre, these could be the best veggie burgers ever!

Ingredients

1 carrot ★ 85g cheese ★ 15g oats ★ 1 large egg ★ 2 teaspoons sesame seeds ★ 2 teaspoons tomato purée ★ $\frac{1}{2}$ teaspoon Cayenne pepper ★ 1 teaspoon mixed herbs ★ 85g wholemeal breadcrumbs ★ a little vegetable oil for frying

You need

grater ★ large bowl ★ wooden spoon ★ plate ★ frying pan ★ spatula

Illustrated by Claire Chrystall

1 Wash the carrot and grate it into a large bowl. Grate the cheese and add it into the bowl.

2 Add the egg, oats, sesame seeds, tomato purée, pepper and herbs to the bowl. Stir with the spoon till everything is really well mixed together. Using your hands, shape the mixture into two burgers.

3 Pour the breadcrumbs onto a plate. Coat the burgers with the breadcrumbs. Press them well in, and make sure you have covered all sides of the burgers.

4 Pour a little oil into the frying pan. Gently fry the burgers on a low heat, until they are golden on the outside and hot on the inside. Turn them carefully with the spatula so they are cooked on both sides.

Be safe

Serve your delicious burgers in a wholemeal roll with a big green salad.

Fruity feast
Get stuck into these sweet treats!

BADGE LINK

Ingredients

6 tablespoons half fat crème fraiche ★ 4 tablespoons brown sugar ★ large knob butter ★ marshmallows ★ a selection of your favourite fruit (grapes, strawberries, bananas, kiwis, apples, oranges and so on)

You need

You need ★ mixing bowl ★ wooden spoon ★ knife ★ chopping board ★ wooden skewers ★ saucepan ★ pastry brush

1 Mix the crème fraiche with two tablespoons of sugar in a bowl until the sugar melts.

2 **Be safe**

Wash your fruit well. Carefully chop apples, bananas and so on into large chunks. Carefully thread the fruit pieces and marshmallows onto wooden skewers. Leave space at each end of the skewers to pick your kebabs up.

3 **Be safe**

Put the butter in the saucepan and melt it over a low heat. Brush a little butter on each kebab. Sprinkle the rest of the sugar on top.

Be safe

4 Grill the kebabs gently until warm throughout – be careful not to let them burn. To serve, put the kebabs on a plate and pour the crème fraiche sauce over the top.

Too busy

Amy and Lauren are at Brownies...

Is the Pack scrapbook finished?

Nearly – just this town map to colour in.

At Amy's house....

Play with me?

Go away Katie – I'm doing the Brownie scrapbook.

This room is a mess. Tidy up before dinner please!

OK, I just have to finish this.

I want it tidy in ten minutes.

Five minutes later...

Can you help me?

In a minute – I told you I'm busy.

Oh Katie, you've made it worse!

Photographs by Laura Ashman

I'd like to send it to the Brownies in Uganda next week.
I could finish it at home.
Thanks Amy, that's really helpful.
Next day...
My sister's such a pain.
I wish I even had a sister.
You don't know how lucky you are!
Katie starts Brownies soon, doesn't she?
Yeah – what a drag!
It's Saturday morning...
You're in the way!
You said we could play football.
Well, I can't now.
I'm helping Dad with the recycling. It's my Good Turn.

Hair-raising!

Liven up your look with these stylish hair ideas.

Twisted

Part your hair in a centre parting. On one side of your head, make another parting exactly halfway down. Above this parting, take the front of the hair and begin to twist it. Twist backwards, adding in more hair as you go, so that the twist lies flat against your head. Finish off with a small band. Now do the same with the hair below the parting. Repeat on the other side of your head, so you end up with four twists.

Wild bunch

Part your hair in a side parting. On the opposite side to the parting, gather a small handful of hair at the front. Tie it in a bunch at the side of your head. On the other side, take a small section from the front of your hair. Plait it and fasten the end with a band.

Zany zig-zag

Use a comb with a long tail to make a zig-zag parting. Start from the front and draw the comb back diagonally for a little way. Now go diagonally the other way. Keep going to make a zig-zag. Then take two small sections from the front of your hair, one on each side. Smooth them back and tie them together at the back of your neck, underneath the rest of your hair.

⭐ On the side

This simple but glamorous do works well with straight or curly hair! Part your hair in a side parting. Brush all your hair over to the other side of your head. Gather it into a bunch and tie with a pretty flower hairband.

⭐ Hair hints

There are lots of simple things you can do to keep your hair in top condition.

★ Eating a healthy diet with plenty of fresh fruit will help your hair stay shiny and healthy.

★ Getting plenty of sleep is important too!

★ If you have to blow-dry your hair, use a low setting on the hairdryer. Don't hold it too close to your head.

★ Have your hair trimmed regularly to keep it tidy and prevent split ends.

⭐ Weaving wonders

Put two high bunches in your hair.

Take a length of ribbon and tie it at the top of one bunch, so that you have one very short end and one long end. Tuck in the short end out of sight. Now plait your hair, weaving the ribbon into the plait. Tie it with a small band at the bottom, then wrap the ribbon around, trim it and tuck in the end. Do the same with the other bunch. To finish off, take two more pieces of ribbon and tie bows at the top.

Whether you're training hard at ballet classes or grooving to the latest hits with your friends, dancing is always fun!

In the groove

Move to the music

All across the world, in every country and culture, people dance. Dancing can express feelings, tell stories, mark special occasions or be part of a religious ceremony. It can also simply be fun! Whatever kind of music you like, there will be a dance you can do. As an added extra, dancing is also really great exercise. So what are you waiting for – get your dancing shoes on!

Getty Images

Tip-top tap

Tap dancing gets its name from the sounds made by the dancers' shoes, which have metal toes and heels. Fast and lively, tap dance began in America. You can tap dance by yourself, but it looks and sounds very spectacular when there are lots of dancers together. Shows and musicals performed in the theatre often have wonderful tap dance routines.

Step in time

Irish dancing has its roots in ancient dance styles, but is getting more and more popular today. It looks very different to other dances, because the dancers hold their arms still by their sides at all times. Their feet move fast though! The dances are made up from complicated steps, kicks and leaps. Dancers wear beautiful costumes with traditional designs on.

Beautiful ballet

Ballet uses music and dance movements to tell stories. Ballet dancers have to be very strong and athletic, but also graceful. They must also be able to mime and express feelings, so the audience can understand the story they are dancing. Ballet dancers often wear elaborate costumes and make-up, especially in traditional ballets like *Swan Lake* or *The Nutcracker*.

AFP/Getty Images

Line up

Line dancing, not surprisingly, is danced in long lines! All the dancers do the same steps together. Modern line dancing has only been around for about 30 years, but it is very popular. You can line dance to many kinds of music, but traditionally American 'Country and Western' music is used. Line dancers often like to dress up in cowboy hats and boots – the more sparkly, the better!

Cool kathak

Kathak is a style of dancing that comes from North India. Graceful movements and the expressions on the dancer's face are both important. The dance is in two parts. It starts with a section of rhythmic movement. Then the dancer uses movement and mime to tell a story. Kathak dancers wear bells on their ankles, which chime in time with the dance.

Dance facts

☆ The haka dance performed by the Maoris of New Zealand was originally a war dance. Now the New Zealand rugby team dance it before their matches!

☆ Michael Flatley, star of the Irish dancing show *Riverdance*, is the world's fastest dancer – he can tap his foot 34 times in one second!

☆ In China, a dragon dance brings good luck and is performed at festivals, especially at the Chinese New Year.

Sixer tip

Ask your Brownie Guider if you can have a dance evening at Brownies. Perhaps someone could come in and teach you line dancing, country dancing or even Hawaiian dancing!

Make this magical treasure island – then grow a palm tree on it!

Treasure island

You need

plastic jar lid, eg from a chocolate spread jar ★ pencil ★ paper plate ★ scissors ★ poster paints ★ matchbox ★ PVA glue and spreader ★ brown tissue paper ★ silver foil, shiny sweet wrappers, sequins, beads ★ knife ★ carrot

 **1** Put the jar lid in the middle of your paper plate and draw round it. Carefully cut out the circle to leave a hole in the plate.

 **2** Turn the paper plate upside down. Draw a wavy shape around the hole in the centre. This will be the island. Paint the island a sandy yellow and the sea round the edges in greeny-blue.

3 To make the treasure chest, take the outside of the matchbox. Cut it along one of the fold lines and flatten out the matchbox. Now cut it in half along the central fold line. You should have two pieces the same size.

4 Stick one of the pieces to the inside part of the matchbox, along the long edge. This makes the lid of the treasure chest.

5 Tear small scraps of brown tissue paper. Spread glue onto the treasure chest and stick on the tissue paper. Cover the inside and outside of the box. Don't worry if it looks a bit crinkly – this will make your treasure chest look ancient.

6 When the glue is dry, fill your treasure chest with treasure! You could use scrunched-up silver foil or sweet wrappers, beads and sequins – anything sparkly! Put a little blob of glue on the island and stick the treasure chest down.

Be safe

7 Now it's time to grow a palm tree! Carefully cut about 2cm off the top of your carrot. Put the carrot top into the jar lid and add a little water, so it comes about halfway up the carrot. Place the paper plate over the jar lid, so the lid is under the hole in the centre.

8 Check the carrot every day and add more water if necessary. In a few days it will have grown into a waving 'tree'!

I want to be...

Check out this A–Z of exciting careers. Then try the quiz to find out which ones might suit you!

Actor: be a star of stage and screen!

Businesswoman: be the boss of your own company!

Carpenter: make beautiful things from wood

Doctor: help ill people to get better

Engineer: work on skyscrapers, planes, spaceships – the sky's the limit!

Fashion designer: create amazing clothes and accessories

Gardener: make lovely outdoor spaces for people to enjoy

Hairstylist: create amazing hairdos for the stars!

IT worker: if you're a computer whizz, this is for you!

Journalist: be first with the news or interview celebrities!

Kennel owner: give dogs a happy holiday home

Lawyer: help people sort out their legal problems

Mechanic: be able to fix things that go wrong!

Nurse: look after people when they're not well

Optician: help people who are having trouble with their eyes

Politician: have your say in running the country!

Queen: OK, so there aren't many opportunities for this career!

Radio producer: organise great music or chat shows!

Singer: would you love to be a pop star?

Teacher: yes, it's school – but you're in charge!

Upholsterer: make and restore soft furniture

Vet: look after sick or injured animals

Writer: could you be the next Jacqueline Wilson?

X: not many careers begin with X!

Youth worker: help young people who are having problems

Zookeeper: look after all sorts of exotic creatures

Do you like to perform?

YES

YES

NO

Are you musical?

Do you like to be in charge?

YES

NO

SINGER

ACTOR

YES

Are you a member of the Royal Family?

NO

YES

Do you like being creative?

QUEEN... MAYBE!

NO

YES

BUSINESSWOMAN POLITICIAN

NO

FASHION DESIGNER JOURNALIST WRITER

Have a think about what you want to be famous for!

START

Do you want to be famous?

NO

YES

Is helping others important to you?

NO

Do you love animals?

Do you like to work with your hands?

YES

YES

NO

Could you help sick or injured animals?

Do you like machinery?

NO

YES

NO

Do you want to work in entertainment?

YES

Would you like to help sick or injured people?

YES

NO

GARDENER
UPHOLSTERER

NO

VET
ZOOKEEPER

KENNEL
OWNER

YES

CARPENTER
MECHANIC

YES

Are you good with computers?

DOCTOR
NURSE
OPTICIAN

NO

HAIRSTYLIST
RADIO
PRODUCER

YES

NO

ENGINEER
IT WORKER

Sixer tip

Is there a career that takes your fancy? Ask your Brownie Guider if someone who does that job could come in and talk to your Pack about it!

LAWYER
TEACHER
YOUTH WORKER

If you know what you want to do, write it here!

Ready, steady, puzzle!

Get ready for action with these great sporting puzzles!

In the swim
Which jigsaw piece completes the puzzle?

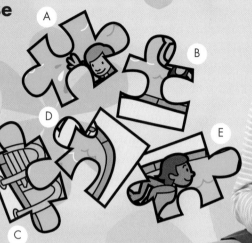

What's my game?
Can you work out what sport each girl likes to play?

Football ★ Squash ★ Netball ★ Snooker

'There are seven people on my team.'

Natalie

Andie

'I use a racquet – but not a tennis racquet!'

'I play a game with 17 balls.'

Chloe

'I score when the ball goes into the net.'

Ruby

Road runner

Can you help the runner find her way to the end of the race?

Illustrated by Andi Good

Pick up sticks

In what order would you have to pick up the hockey sticks so that you take the top one each time?

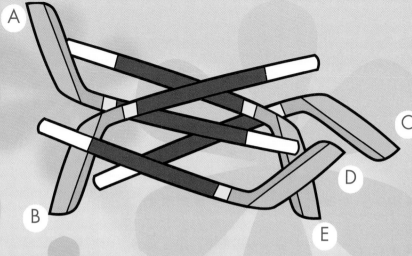

Scrambled sports

Find two different sports in each line.

HORCUKEGBYY

NDEITVBIANLGL

TFEOONNTIBASLL

SCQRUIACKSEHT

SKSNAOTOKINEGR

SRWOIUMNDEMIRNSG

Name of the game

Rearrange these letters to make the name of a sport. How many words can you make using the letters?

odd ball

One of these footballs is different from the rest. Can you spot it?

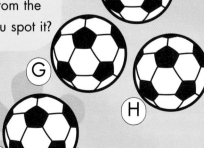

How well did you do? Check the answers on page 77.

Guides: the top ten

Check out these ten fantastic reasons for being a Guide!

Patrols

Guides belong to Patrols, which are a bit like Sixes. A Patrol is a group of friends that plan and do activities together. Of course they have a lot of fun at the same time!

The G file

A handy personal organiser, packed with all there is to know about Guides. It has record pages to fill in and a calendar with stickers. Great for busy Guides with lots to think about!

Go For Its!

Guides choose what to do from these exciting activity packs. Each one has a different theme. For example, there is *Go For It! Football*, *Go For It! Animal active* and even *Go For It! Chocolate!*

The clothes

Guides get to choose from a range of trendy tops. They can wear whatever they like on the bottom half!

Camp or holiday

Guides just love going away together. They might camp out, stay in a holiday house or even go abroad. Wherever they go, they always have a great time!

Patrols like to get together at a Patrol member's house for a sleepover. Videos, pizza, makeovers, chat – what could be more fun?

Badges

Just like Brownies, Guides have all sorts of great badges to do. Would you like to try the Circus skills, Holiday or Party planner badges?

Pack Leader

Older Guides can choose to help out at a Brownie or Rainbow unit. They might help the unit leaders by organising games or lending a hand with crafts.

Unit Guidelines

The Guides decide on their own rules for how the unit is run. Everybody gets a say, then all the Guides and leaders sign the Guidelines.

Baden-Powell challenge

This is the biggest adventure for Guides! It's a chance to choose and organise a whole range of fun activities.

You decide

What do you think is the best thing about Guides? Rate these ideas from one to ten.

Pick the one that you think would be most fun, and write '1' in the star.

Then go through the rest and put them all in order.

Whatever order you put them in, you now know ten reasons why Guides are great!

Light lunches

Cook up a feast for you and a friend, with these tasty lunch recipes!

Hot hot dogs!

Spice up an ordinary hot dog with a zingy tomato sauce!

Ingredients

1 small red onion ★ small tin of chopped tomatoes ★ 1 teaspoon caster sugar ★ pinch of chilli powder ★ pinch of salt and pepper ★ 2 sausages ★ 30g cheese ★ 2 long rolls or chunks of French bread

You need

knife ★ chopping board ★ bowl ★ teaspoon

Illustrated by Martina Farrow

1 To make the spicy tomato sauce, chop the onion into very small pieces and put it in the bowl.

Be safe

2 Add the tomatoes, sugar, salt, pepper and chilli powder. Mix together well.

3 Now put the grill on a medium heat and cook the sausages. Make sure they are well cooked.

Be safe

4 Slice the cheese and lay the slices inside the rolls or French bread. Carefully put the hot sausages in too. Spoon plenty of tomato sauce over the sausages. Serve your hot dogs with a crisp green salad, and enjoy!

Perfect pittas

Pitta breads stuffed with a crunchy cheesy filling – delicious!

Ingredients

100g Cheddar cheese ★ 50g chopped nuts ★ 50g raisins ★ 2 sticks of celery ★ 1 apple ★ 2 tablespoons natural yoghurt or mayonnaise ★ 2 pitta breads ★ a few lettuce leaves

You need

knife ★ chopping board ★ large bowl ★ tablespoon

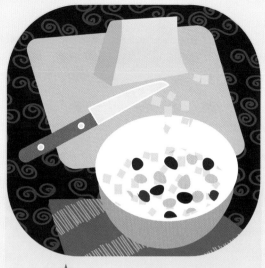

1 Carefully chop the cheese into small cubes. Put them into the bowl. Add the nuts and raisins

Be safe

2 Wash the celery sticks and cut off the leafy ends. Chop the celery into small pieces. Put them into the bowl.

3 Wash the apple and cut it into quarters. Carefully cut the core off each apple quarter. Chop the apple into small cubes and add them to the bowl.

4 Add the yoghurt or mayonnaise to the bowl. Stir it well so that everything is mixed together.

5 Be safe

Put the grill on a low heat, and gently warm the pitta breads. Split them open carefully – they will have hot steam inside. Put one or two lettuce leaves into each pitta bread. Now stuff them with your cheese salad, and eat!

Answers

Fab friends (page 9)

Super secret
The messages say:
'Hi Jo, can you come over after Brownies? Love Ella.'
'Dear Ella, I would love to come over. See you later, Jo.'

Animal planet
Africa = giraffe; Antarctica = penguin; Asia = panda; Australasia = kangaroo; Europe = red squirrel; North America = raccoon; South America = llama

Riddle me this
The country is FRANCE.

Map maker
Piece C will complete the map.

Go global! (pages 16-17)

Wordsearch

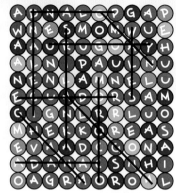

On holiday
Ellie is going to New Zealand.
Mia is going to Sweden.
Jodi is going to Egypt.
Sarah is going to Canada.

Flying the flag
A and C are exactly alike.

Crossed countries

World of colour (page 29)

Try this
The ink in the pen is actually made from several different colours, called pigments. Some pigments are made from smaller, lighter particles than others. These spread out faster and travel further up the paper than the pigments made from bigger, heavier particles.

Miss Dorothy (page 33)

1. All these things can be recycled.

2. a. True
b. False – people in countries like Denmark, Switzerland and Japan recycle loads more than we do.
c. True
d. True
e. False – some charities take old mobiles.
f. True
g. False – kitchen foil can't go in can banks.

3. Switch off the light when you leave the room.
Save trees – buy recycled paper.
Walk or cycle on short journeys – don't go in the car.
Help birds by feeding them in winter.
Save water – turn off dripping taps.

Creature feature (pages 34-35)

Looks a bit fishy! There are 32 fish in the pond.

Wild wordsearch

Dinner time!

Stripy types
Numbers 4 and 5 are identical.

Home sweet home
Flopsy lives in burrow A.
Mopsy lives in burrow C.
Topsy lives in burrow B.

Long story
Frog, deer, moth, rat, mole, toad, owl.

Brownie brain-teasers (pages 52-53)

Sweet treats

Puppy puzzler
Daisy belongs to Carrie.
Chester belongs to Emma.
Snowy belongs to Rosie.

Odd sock
Matching pairs: A and D; B and G; C and I; F and H. E is the odd one.

Helping hand

Top of the shops
Oranges – Rice – Tomatoes – Yoghurt – Biscuits – Spaghetti

What's the word? PROMISE

Ready, steady, puzzle! (pages 70-71)

In the swim
Piece A completes the puzzle.

Road runner

What's my game?
Natalie plays netball.
Andie plays squash.
Chloe plays snooker.
Ruby plays football.

Pick up sticks
You would have to pick up the sticks in the order: D, B, A, E, C.

Name of the game
The sport is BADMINTON.

Scrambled sports
Hockey – rugby
Netball – diving
Tennis – football
Squash – cricket
Skating – snooker
Swimming – rounders

Odd ball
Ball C is the odd one out.